C000043610

THE HOUR

ANA BLANDIANA

The Hour of Sand

SELECTED POEMS 1969–1989

Translated by Peter Jay & Anca Cristofovici

ANVIL PRESS POETRY

First published in 1990
by Anvil Press Poetry Ltd
69 King George Street London SE10 8PX
Second edition 1990
Copyright © Ana Blandiana 1990
Translations and introduction
copyright © Peter Jay and Anca Cristofovici 1990

This book is published
with financial assistance from
The Arts Council

Designed and composed by Anvil
Photoset in Palatino by Wordstream
Printed in England
by Morganprint Blackheath Ltd

British Library Cataloguing in Publication Data

Blandiana, Ana, 1942–
  The hour of sand: selected poems 1969–1989. –2nd ed.
  I. Title   II. Jay, Peter, 1945–   III. Cristofovici, Anca, 1956–
859'.134

ISBN 0 85646 240 3

ACKNOWLEDGEMENTS

Some of these translations have appeared in *Invisible City*
(USA), *Secolul 20* (Bucharest), *The Sunday Times*, *The Times
Literary Supplement* and the anthology *Writing from the World*
(University of Iowa Press, 1976).

    Peter Jay thanks Hazel Wilson for her help with some early
versions, and Andrea Deletant for her collaboration on drafts
of fifteen poems.

    We are grateful to the Central and East European
Publishing Project for a grant which enabled us to complete
work on the translations.

Contents

Introduction

ANA BLANDIANA is one of Romania's most admired and prominent poets. Her early poems appeared in the review *Tribuna* in 1959, when she was seventeen. A few years later, her debut collection *First Person Plural* (1964) was greeted with widespread critical acclaim. Since then she has published eleven collections of poetry, as well as several volumes of essays, fiction, children's books and translations. Her delicate, subtle and pointed poetry has gained her a huge readership at home, where she has received awards from the Romanian Academy and Writers' Union.

Ana Blandiana was born in 1942, in the Transylvanian town Timişoara. She went to school in Oradea and university in Cluj, where she took a degree in Romance philology and literature. She then moved to Bucharest, working as editor of the students' review *Amfiteatru*, and as a librarian at the Institute of Fine Arts, before becoming a full-time writer. With a few interruptions caused by circumstances beyond her control, she wrote a regular column for the Bucharest weekly *România Literară* from 1974 to 1988. She is married to the writer and film critic Romulus Rusan.

The year of Blandiana's debut, 1964, was the annus mirabilis of post-war Romanian poetry. Many poets published their first books at this auspicious moment in Ceauşescu's honeymoon period after the years of Stalinism: Nichita Stănescu, Marin Sorescu, Ioan Alexandru, and – belatedly – poets of a slightly older generation who had been unable to publish in the fifties, such as Ştefan Aug. Doinaş. Among these poets, who have taken strikingly divergent paths, Blandiana has developed a mature voice which preserves the spontaneity of youth, its capacity of wonder and its often forthright, challenging approach to current issues.

She is not, in technical literary terms, an innovator. Her 'structure', the poet Mircea Ivănescu wrote in 1977, 'is that of a Romantic so wounded by what she senses as disintegration and impurity in her contact with the actual, that is to say with the flow, with the passage of time, that she chooses to live her nostalgias for original purity, for memory (whether or not with anecdotal connections to her own life), for inner experiences as the more authentic.' The charismatic obsolescence often resonant in her poetry is the reflex of a nostalgic sensibility, but one that has defined its targets very precisely. Even at its most personal, as in her love poems, her poetry is never confessional, but her vulnerability plays an important rôle. Rather than try to hide this, she has chosen to use it positively as a natural and authentic form of experience, a risk which is typical of her commitment to the imagination. This authenticity is the key to her popularity. Both the vividness of her writing and the reality of the values it embodies strike deep and common chords in the Romanian psyche.

Romania is a crossroads country, both geographically, historically and perhaps spiritually. A buffer zone between east and west, and a non-industrial society until the late 1940s, it had a strong tradition of trying to maintain the continuity of ancestral values and to remould them in accordance with the fluctuations of the present. Elements of this kind of traditionalism, strongly in evidence in the poetry of Lucian Blaga (1895–1961) and in a different way in that of Nichita Stănescu (1933–1983), have been a constant thread in modern Romanian literature. Ana Blandiana has rediscovered it in an undiluted form, thus distinguishing herself from most of the poets of her generation who are more willing to embrace formal innovation. Yet she treats it very personally. Her achievement has been to live this tradition and to make it live in her poetry as though it was absolutely fresh. In this she expresses fundamental values which have a specific resonance and relevance in the Romanian context.

What is surprising about Blandiana's poetry, coming

from a country with a long tradition of literary experiment, is that its premises are so unashamedly Romantic. Even in her wildest flights, the tone is intimate and quite unembarrassed. But the Romantic vision so evident in her poems is one that is responsive to present-day conditions, and this is especially clear in her poems of the past five or six years. While she is incapable of the cynicism and sarcasm of some of her contemporaries, she can write harshly discordant poems such as 'Late', 'With My Face Toward the Mountains' and 'Scene'. These, and indeed all the poems which we have chosen from her latest book, could only have been written by a convinced Romantic who feels that fundamental values are under direct threat.

Hers is a poetry of epiphanies. But they are not the well-turned, minor personal epiphanies of everyday life in which so much contemporary poetry deals. Rather, they are examples or intimations of deeper, more secret and subterranean intimacies between her and the ritual cycles of life, to whose infinitesimal vibrations she listens with longing. Her sense of nature is not idyllic, since it embraces natural violence and terror; rather, it is the essential, historic and common element through which people can aspire to pure communion or harmony with the world and in themselves. Blandiana inherits this sense of nature partly from the animistic world of Romanian folk poetry and fairy tale, partly from her own childhood and the values of her upbringing.

Sleep, the meeting-ground of dream and nightmare, of atavistic impulses and present concerns, and the halfway house between life and death, has a pervasive presence in her poems. She is a lyric poet rather than a myth-maker, but her poems often have the force of legend or folklore. Her poetic sensibility has obvious links, thematic and tonal, with that of Romania's national poet, the visionary Romantic Mihai Eminescu (1856–1889). It is an unusual achievement to have brought Eminescian traits back into contemporary poetry, for his fluid and beautiful verses, learned by heart by every schoolchild, have long run the risk of cliché. Her appropriation of Eminescu's tone is not abstract and refined like that of Nichita Stănescu, but concrete, almost to the level of quotation, in phrasing, rhyme patterns and even grammatical constructions. For example, a particular use of reflexives which is immediately recognized by Romanian readers as characteristic of Eminescu occurs sometimes together with an imperative: 'deep / May the moon reflect / In the next life' is how we have inadequately rendered 'adînc / Răsfrînge-se luna / În viaţa cealaltă' ('How I Could Have Wished'), or through metaphoric transference of an impersonal reflexive verb, 'a se întuneca' (to grow dark), to the first person in a special instance of the future perfect: 'după ce / Mă voi fi întunecat', 'until after / I have gone into the dark' at the end of 'Star Borne on the Wind'. These examples also illustrate the loss of certain kinds of special nuance which poetry must suffer in translation.

The qualities of Ana Blandiana's poetry are easier to define in personal rather than in literary terms. They have a lightness of touch which comes with the confidence in her commitment. They have unobtrusive wit and formal elegance, and they can penetrate very sharply indeed. Their props – angels, butterflies and so on – are quite her own, though they could be examined in the light of a long line of such creatures in Romanian poetry from Eminescu, through Vasile Voiculescu (1884–1963) to Nichita Stănescu and a host of contemporaries.

Behind her neo-Romanticism, a strong religious or spiritual impulse informs Blandiana's poetry. The daughter of a priest, she inherits the tradition of Transylvanian poets who were writing, as has been said, 'in the shadow of the church', most of them heavily censored and read in secret in Blandiana's youth. Like the poet and philosopher Lucian Blaga, she is absorbed in the search for a communicable form of interior salvation, as for example in 'Inside'. She often focuses on small (from the human standpoint) details

– grains, seeds, cells, stars – and, without straining for effect, expands them to visionary landscapes: the ending of 'You Never See the Butterflies' is worthy of Samuel Palmer. She is closely attentive to the mysteries of growth and change. Even in her fascination with purity (clear waters, limpid sounds, transparent figures) in the shadow of mortality (rottenness, mud), there are metamorphoses: processes of disintegration are also processes of purification, as in the distillation of alcohols in 'I Feel Sleepy'. In her later work, these processes are more stark and startling, as her preoccupation has increasingly been with bearing witness to the more blatantly destructive forces of change, those which threaten to disrupt existing harmonies, however fragile, in the rhythms of existence. In a poem like 'Late' – originally titled 'Star of Prey' – Nature itself is seen as contaminated by the false: it has become mere scenery, a travesty of itself. The stamp of this devastating awareness is imprinted on all her poems published over the past few years.

Blandiana's presence in the Romanian literary world is strong, yet somewhat distanced from its main trends. Her newspaper columns (akin to prose poetry, a long-standing genre in Romanian literary journalism) manifest the same spirit as her poetry. Her stance is exemplary, her voice consistent and firm. It is a necessary voice anywhere in these times, but especially in the Romania whose readers she addresses. Bucharest is still in some ways an 'Oriental Town' – one of her few poems to borrow a tone from the symbolist, George Bacovia (1881–1957) – a capital whose life retains something of the structure of a village, and where poets command more public respect than in the western democracies. It is a place where books are devoured like bread, where publicity or print-runs have little to do with a book's popularity, which is rather a matter of hearsay and of sharing. Literature is a collective refuge, a way of survival. In the strategies of this survival, Blandiana has been a model of unswerving consciousness.

We have borrowed our title and chosen most of the poems here from *Ora de nisip* (The Hour of Sand), published by Editura Eminescu in 1983. This was an extensive selection from Ana Blandiana's previous books together with a section of new poems, most of which were included in *Stea de pradă* (Star of Prey: Cartea Românească, 1985). Our selection ends with poems from the section of uncollected poems in *Poezii* (Poems: Editura Minerva, 1989). These form part of a new collection, *Arhitectura valurilor* (The Architecture of Waves), which was planned for publication in 1989 but has not yet appeared.

We have tried in these versions to be true to the words as well as to the spirit of her poems. Our translations were made in close consultation, and we bear joint responsibility for them. Our aim was to make a representative cross-section of poems from all the phases of the large body of Blandiana's work, choosing both poems that we liked and that we felt could stand transplantation. For this reason, we have chosen perhaps fewer of her rhymed stanzaic poems than we would have liked. We are grateful to Ana Blandiana for her suggestions about the selection, her patience with our detailed questions and her encouragement of the translation.

PETER JAY
ANCA CRISTOFOVICI

Greenwich – Paris
August 1989

The Hour of Sand

Nealegere

Adusă la marea judecată
Care se termină prin trimiterea pe pămînt,
Eu, găsită nevinovată,
Am primit dreptul
Să mă aleg pe mine.
Dar nu bărbat, şi nu femeie,
Şi nici un animal n-am vrut să fiu,
Şi nici o pasăre, şi nici o plantă.
Se-aud secundele căzînd
Din marele drept de-a alege.
Se-aud lovindu-se de piatră:
Nu, nu, nu, nu.
Zadarnic adusă la judecată,
Zadarnic nevinovată.

Non-choice

Brought to the great judgement
That ends with the sending to earth,
I, found innocent,
Have been given the right
To choose myself.
But neither man, nor woman,
Nor an animal did I want to be,
Nor a bird, or plant.
The seconds are heard dropping
From the great right to choose.
They are heard breaking against rock:
No, no, no, no.
In vain brought to the judgement,
In vain innocent.

Ties

Everything is I myself.
Give me a leaf that doesn't look like me,
Help me find an animal
That doesn't moan with my voice.
Wherever I tread the earth splits,
And I see the dead who bear my image
Embracing and begetting other dead.
Why so many ties with the world,
So many parents and enforced descendants
And all this lunatic likeness?
The universe haunts me with a thousand faces of mine
And my only defence is to hit out at myself.

The Closed Eye

I don't dare close my eyes an instant
for fear
of crushing the world between my eyelids,
of hearing it crack noisily
like a hazelnut between the teeth.
How much longer can I steal from sleep?
How much longer can I keep it alive?
I look on in despair
and pity like a dog
the helpless universe
that will disappear within my closed eye.

The North

We do not cheat out of meanness,
But from lack of skill.
Fogged, we no longer know
Who we are and how.
Behind, a row of unknown parents,
Before, a row of unknown sons.
What do we know? Who do we know?
Insecure we move:
We take one step, then another,
And another, and set out at last
Looking nostalgically in the opposite direction . . .
If we just had the answer to one question:
Where is the north?
The hair on our foreheads quivers lightly,
In the wind aroused
By the passing of time.

Old Hermits

Grown old, the hermits in the woods,
The wolf-fur stuck to their bodies,
Hair weaving their eyes
Closing up their ears,
And in their tangled beards bees make hives.
They can't remember why they came here
And long since have not known the word
That they were meant to cry out to the world.
A sign of heaven's will is sent to them
Now and then, in the guise of a vulture,
But the old men play
Plaiting flowers in the bird's feathers
While God, angered, does not understand
That they've forgotten how to hate.

Condition

I
am like
sand in the hourglass
which
can be time
only
in
falling

Fall

The prophets in the desert have died out
And angels with drooping wings
Are led in columns
And gathered in the squares.
They'll soon be judged.
They'll be asked: what sin
Has chased their beings from the heavens?
What guilt? What trespass? What betrayal?
With their final love,
They'll look at us with sleep-misted eyes
And will not find the devilish daring
To avow that why angels fall
Is not sin, not sin,
But tiredness.

Let Us Let the Words Fall

Let us let the words fall
Only like fruit, only like leaves,
Only those in which death ripened.
Let us let them fall
Almost rotten,
With their flesh just clothing
The sacred bone.
Loosened, the bare core,
Like the moon from withered clouds,
Might steal perhaps towards the earth . . .

The Soul

The soul is something within us
That cannot exist outside.
How often has it happened
That I've discovered
Bare souls in the grass, about to die . . .
I took them into my palm carefully,
But could never
Find anyone quickly enough
Who would take them in,
I felt the hollow of my palm bare
And a haze, untouched by leaves, slipping
Distrustfully through my body.
Does the soul shelter within us
From God?

Do You Remember the Beach?

Do you remember the beach
Covered with bitter shards
On which
We could not walk barefoot?
The way in which
You gazed at the sea
And said you were listening to me?
Do you recall
The hysterical gulls
Spinning in the toll
Of bells from unseen churches
With banners of fish,
The way in which
You were running away
Towards the sea
Shouting to me that you needed
Distance
To look at me?
The snow
Was going out
Mingled with birds
In the water,
With an almost joyful desperation
I watched
Your footprints on the sea
And the sea
Closed like an eyelid
Over the eye in which I was waiting.

About the Country We Come From

Let's talk
About the country we come from.
I come from summer,
A delicate homeland
Which any leaf,
Falling, can put out,
But the sky is so heavy with stars
That it sometimes hangs down to the earth
And if you come close, you can hear the grass
Tickling the stars in laughter,
And the flowers are so many
That your orbits dried as if by sun
Hurt,
And round suns hang
From every tree;
Where I come from
All that's missing is death,
There's so much happiness
It almost sends you to sleep.

If We Killed One Another

If we killed one another
Gazing into our eyes,
Into each other's eyes round which
The lashes are like a crown of thorns
Conclusively wreathing
Any glance,
If we killed each other, after gazing
Into our eyes with boundless love,
And, knowing you, I'd say:
Die,
Die, my dear,
How good that will be,
You'll stay just with me,
Born from the word
You'll know the taste of earth,
Weave them in your hands, and feel
The roots, how beautiful,
In the uncomprehended joy
Of being no more throughout eternity . . .
And, stroking me, you'd say:
Die, my dear,
My love with the October brow
Framed as in icons
By death's round halo,
Die, and leave
Your colours to the flowers, bequeath
Your long locks to the paths, your eyes
A brilliance for the seas,
Then you'll know
Where to go
To find them, when you come . . .

If we died together suddenly
Both of us killer and victim,
Saviour and saved,
Gazing into our eyes endlessly,
Long after we could see no more . . .

White Bodies of Poplars
Coming Out of the Water

White bodies of poplars coming out of the water
With sleepy, slender forms,
Beautiful adolescents or maybe women,
Sweet confusion, moist locks
Not daring to hide desire,
Round, unending the water,
The moon pouring oil
On its glitter.
We walked barefoot, unruffled,
And I felt
My fingers fallen asleep in your hand,
So much love was on the waters
That we could not sink,
So much silence, that time
Would not dare to tell one second,
The sky voice any cloud,
Water mumble a wave,
Only our bare feet
Stepping on the moonlight
Uttered a slight sound.

Mother

Mother, my first tomb,
A blazing darkness
Forsaken with such foolish impatience
When every lump
Of its clay
Resisted that departure without sense.
Will you ever forgive my resurrection,
The hasty resurrection tearing me from you
So that, from light to light,
I could be drawn to yet another death?
It's getting colder still,
The foreignness steals into me,
As I climb, the road back sweeps itself away.
It's such a distance to you,
That churches could be raised
To mediate the prayers between us.

Teach Me How to Burn Darkly

Let me light myself from your darkness,
In the fierce light
Teach me how to burn darkly,
Mould my flame
In the shape of wings
And purify it of all colour.
Or,
Better still,
Give me a seed of darkness
To bury in the ground
And turn the seasons faster
To make it grow,
For me to sow it afresh.
In the fierce light
There would then be woods and pastures,
Groves, orchards, meadows and night forests,
A tender pitch-dark
In which we could die whenever we like,
A darkness in which
We would no longer be kind, or beautiful,
But simply alone,
And, no longer having to look,
Closing our eyes, we would be able to see.

Our Place

Our place is not here.
Vainly we are trying to rot away —
Pips from us,
As many as in pomegranates,
Will not find enough
Earth to make them sprout.
We are not dying yet,
We still have
That brightness to endure
Which lets us journey through it
Asleep and deafened with dreams,
Our place
Is somewhere further on,
Or perhaps it has passed
Unrecognized by us.

You Never See the Butterflies

You never see
The butterflies, how they look at each other above us?
Nor the signs that the wind
Makes to the grass as we walk by?
If I suddenly turn,
The branches are struck dumb
And wait for us to move on.
Haven't you noticed the birds are setting?
Haven't you noticed the leaves are going out?
Haven't you noticed the whispers
Growing on our backs,
Like moss on the side of tree-trunks facing north?
And the silence waiting for us everywhere . . .
They all know something which is hidden from us.
We are sentenced perhaps.
On our heads there's a high price.
At night the stars shine aroused
When the rattle of corn-ears is heard.

Trees Had Eyes Once

Trees had eyes once,
I could swear,
I know for sure
That when I was a tree I could see,
I remember being in wonder
At the peculiar wings of birds
As they passed in front of me,
But whether the birds guessed
My eyes,
I can no longer tell.
Now I look in vain for the eyes of trees.
Perhaps I cannot see them
Because I'm a tree no more,
Or perhaps they've gone down through their roots
Into the ground,
Or perhaps
Who knows
So it seemed only to me
And trees have been blind from the beginning . . .
But then why
When to them I come close
Do I feel how
They follow me with their glances
In a familiar way,
Why, when they rustle and blink
With their thousands of eyelids,
Do I feel like shouting –
What have you seen? . . .

I Dream Sometimes My Body

I dream sometimes my body
Caught in nets, wrinkles,
And dragged through snow
On the frozen, glittering beach
Of a limpid sea,
I never see the fisherman
But I know that he's your father,
I see only the net of wrinkles
And my body, a rich
Catch.
Tenderly I dream that morning of death
With its clean, unknown silence
When you no longer come,
When I no longer call you
And everything falls asleep with open eyes,
And only, light within light, an echo,
Flickers a faint curse –
Let the net unravel,
Let me slide again
Into the water without time or stain.

I'm Like a Horse's Eye

I'm like a horse's eye
Blinkered towards the world.
When I reach you,
Don't ask me
What trees and what flowers
I've met.
I see only the road
And from time to time
The shadows of clouds,
Transmitting me messages
That I don't understand.

The Mist Descending

The mist descending
Is it your eyelid
Closing sleepily over the world?
Does the world
Dream beyond it, and
Have only I been forgotten
Awake
Just so
That I may see how sleep
Runs into death,
Fine, unchanging,
Like a spring
Setting in the sea,
Like stars that set
Slowly, slowly contained by the sun?
That I may see how limpid death,
From time to time,
Is clouded as it dreams,
That I have been forgotten awake
Just so
That your eyelid descending
Touchingly over the world
Might hurt me? . . .

Oh, Your Body

Oh, your body I can see it through ink,
Ink muddying us even in our sleep
Like sour, animal sweat.
I want to reach you
And my fingers slip,
I cannot see you now,
I can barely hear you,
Tell me, tell me again
That the whirlpool into which I sink
Darkens us in the same way.
I call you
But, violently as from a wound,
The ink springs up between us.
Will you still know me, wait for me,
Let me back,
Take me in
From the blue-black mud?
Will you cross
Blue plains again,
Desert seas,
Mute, in tears
For me to offer you
A mouth quivering towards a kiss
With lips blue-blackened by words?

Keep Your Eyes Closed

Keep your eyes closed, keep your eyes closed,
Once only are we given.
I ask you nothing.
The snowfall spreads,
Has buried graveyard and village,
Walls the church in,
Only the tops of poplars
Sprout above like grass.
The snowfall spreads and rises
Like a leavened plain
That soon will stop
Time falling from above.
Keep your eyes closed,
Once only are we given
And we must give but once.
I ask you nothing; wait
For the last time-flake to set
And the heavens to fill with emptiness
And peace, only then
Remove your left arm from the nails
And slowly overturn the clock with snow.

I Feel Sleepy

I feel sleepy as
Fruits in autumn feel,
I feel sleepy, I feel fine,
I'm good and I'm warm,
Bees are humming
In my mind,
My head will tumble on my shoulder
Soon,
Just as any fruit
Comes to fall one day
And starts to rot
On its earthward side.
I nod off
And my head
Rots with dreams,
Gently, sweet
Alcohols distil,
A worm-angel nods off in his turn
And starts to dream
Rotting.

Between Worlds

I pass from one life into another
Lightly stroking
The mane of the sleep-lion
At the entrance,
Accustomed to me
And my eternal disappearance at dawn,
My eternal crepuscular
Returns.
Defeated, sometimes
I no longer manage to reach him.
Then he rises,
Takes my head in his teeth
With tenderness
And drags me slowly.
Other times I no longer
Know how to return from the dream.
Then he starts after me
In the labyrinth,
Tells me with a roar
That he will save me,
To wait without moving
In remembrance,
For him to find
And bring me
To his kingdom.
Oh, his wonderful kingdom,
A thin land,
A tender boundary
Of the hour
Between two worlds that devour themselves
Tearing each and the other apart
Ceaselessly.

Perhaps Someone Is Dreaming Me

Perhaps someone is dreaming me –
That's why my gestures
Are so soft
And unfinished,
With their aim forgotten
Half-way,
Grotesquely,
That's why my outlines get blurred
Second by second
And my deeds melt . . .
And perhaps the one who's dreaming me
From time to time is plucked
From sleep,
Awoken,
Carried by force into
His true life,
That's why I darken
Suspended sometimes
As from a thread that melts with snow,
Without knowing
If he will ever fall asleep again
So that something might happen to me
Again.

Poem

Who shall dream and what,
In the time heaped over us –
Snowdrifts heavy with sleep
Through which move
Sleepwalking heroes
With gestures slow and brave?
Don't scream,
They die if woken,
It's enough to cry
To see them –
Stillundeath's
So shy
Tokens.

Country

Within you I yearn for no one,
Earth set in sleep
Through green orbits,
And I'm foreign if I cross the boundary
Of your tired locks.
Your language alone
I know how to speak in dreams
And to tell fairy-tales only for you
My too transient paradise,
My too transient lord.
It's cold outside
And there's a thick fog,
Night closes in,
Time comes down slowly,
But it's so fine and warm at home
When we are one another's country.

It Snows with Enmity

It snows with enmity,
With hatred the snow falls
On the waters frozen with hatred,
On the orchards blossomed from evil,
On the bedevilled birds who endure.
It snows as if through snow
The life of this aquatic people
Should come to an end,
It snows with a human
Relentlessness,
Poisonously it snows.
Who would be surprised?
Only I still know
That snow
Was love in the beginning.
It's so late
And it snows hideously,
And all I can think of
Is that I should wait
For the famished wolves,
And be some use to them.

Churches Don't Have Roofs

Churches don't have roofs,
But shingle wings
Shrivelled on their bodies,
And a time will come
When they will open them
And rise
Slowly, as if grudgingly,
Carrying their beings
Of gold and smoke
Higher and higher in the air,
Flying with a huge roar, like
A flock of heavy birds
Towards sunset,
While the hysterical mountains,
Mixed with the sea
Gushing towards them,
Would tumble –
A beautiful end for the world
Under the live blue sky
Swarming with huge live churches.

Oriental Town

With sap oozed on the streets
Oriental town in the plain,
With a sun that shamelessly
Sips up its sordid prey,

Liquefied town, boiling river,
Ferocious aromas that rise
Up to the fruit-sky where
The very last thought decays.

Who Named

Who named
This colour
In the ecstasy of leaves
Gold,
This triumphant
No man's land
Between life and death,
This beatitude
Enveloping the earth
In its vegetal light,
With fragrance of fruit
Stripped on branches
And a virginal,
Heavy indecency?
Who dared
Give a word
To the clearest,
Deepest namelessness
That we flow toward,
Unworthy of so much hope,
All of us, among
Wise grape-clusters
And thin, prankish twigs?
Be quiet!
Be quiet and listen to
The syllables of grass rustling
Drily in light –
Not even they
Dare speak the name
Of this final kingdom.

In Sleep

Crickets make their music only in sleep,
Crickets by day are only insects,
Let them slumber, grasses, and hide them
From the suspect sincerities of day;

From the parched and futile truth
Shield them, most limpid lord of dew,
May everything they fail to live
Come to pass for them in sleep;

Let them slumber bound in nightmares,
Playing their own ropes like strings,
Thin princes of shriek sacrificed shrilly
To the solitudes of the moon.

From There

From there, from the leaf
Another looks at me
With a patience divided into summers and autumns,
Without saying a thing,
Just wondering
At my eyes closed towards him.

Oh, on my eyelids grass sprang up,
And it was green, and it parched
Since when they stopped rising outwards,
My lashes bogged down
In knots and tangles,
Since when my eyes
Don't cease to look at me

Under the green ray
In which the leaf's glance bathes me
As in the depth of an ever-patient sea,
Without saying a thing,
Only preparing me
For harsher, longer resurrections.

Vestment

Sometimes in the morning
I wake up frozen
And, still half asleep,
I pull, drowsy and shivering,
My young, warm, silky
Body over myself.
I wrap myself in it
Teeth chattering childishly,
Happy that for one more day,
One whole day
I will be
In a shelter from eternity.

Flight

You don't die
From the illness that I suffer,
You live –
Its substance is pure eternity,
A kind of cancer of time
Multiplying from itself ceaselessly.
It's an impeccable illness,
A perpetual suffering like a glass vowel
Laminated in the deafening air,
A fall
Which, only because it's without end,
We call flight.

Loneliness

Loneliness is a town
In which the rest have died,
The streets are clean,
The squares empty,
Everything's suddenly seen
Dilated in the desert
So clearly fated.
Loneliness is a town
Where it snows tremendously
And not a footstep
Desecrates the light
Settled in layers,
And only you, the wakeful eye
Open above those who sleep,
Watch, understand, and never get tired
Of so much silence and immaculacy
In which no one struggles
And no one is deceived,
Where even the forsaken animal's tear
Is too clear
To hurt.
In the valley
Between suffering and death,
Loneliness is a town that's happy.

The File

Words cross the road
Like a file of orphans
From the Children's Home,
Each with a fist clenched
On the coat of the one in front,
Their only care
Not to be cut off
One from another.

So Cold

I am so cold,
That I think the only
Way I could still be saved
Would be like those who, frozen,
Were stitched inside
The bellies of animals
To warm themselves
And well muffled up
In the pained coat of fur,
Caked in the blood of beasts
Came into the world once more.
Too far from
The flames of hell,
In my angelic loneliness
I froze,
But who would be
Able to open their ribs up
To receive me?

Armour

My body
Is only the armour
An archangel chose
In which to pass through the world
And, so disguised,
Wings parcelled up
Inside,
The visor of a smile
Shut tight on his face,
He enters the thick of battle,
Lets himself be accosted with smut,
Splattered with glances,
And even stroked
On the cold mail of his skin
Under which repulsion hatches
The exterminating angel.

Hunting

I have never run after words,
All I have sought
Was their long
Silver shadows,
Dragged by the sun through grass
Or drawn by the moon over the sea;
I have never hunted
Anything but the shadows of words –
It is very skilful hunting
Learned from old people
Who know
That within a word
Nothing is more precious
Than its shadow
And they no longer have a shadow,
The words that have sold their souls.

Proofs

Angels hit by stones
Who still have the strength
Not to draw back into the air
Beg me, wounded
And exhausted, for hospitality
And still fluttering lightly
Fall asleep meek and delicate in my notebooks,
Pulling just in slumber
When they become chilly
A white sheet over their wings.
In the morning I know I've not been dreaming
Because of the feathers' impression on the pages
And I hurry to memorize them
Before they're confiscated from me
In order to decree new species
Of birds of prey.

Camouflage

Could we ask of paradise
More than that it should be like
A swallow's nest?
On the inside
Immaculate, radiant,
Lined with feathers
As of angels,
On the outside
Rough clay,
A perfect camouflage
Which we call –
With such precaution –
Death.

In Memoriam

How will the wind
Be able
To shake the stars
In the autumn;
How will the autumn
Be able
To shrivel the stars
In the sky;
How will the sky
Be able
To stumble
Because of time's passage
And fall on its snout;
How will time
Be able
To pass
Out?

Eleusis

Everything ends with an ear of wheat
Shown to the crowd on the steps of the temple
Screening the mysteries.
Oh, we could have rolled
Onto the cold slabs that were struck by bodies
Still alive, still alive,
Gripped by desire and hatred in turn,
Loving or fighting,
The same unbridled struggle
That demands more than it hopes for,
When we all know
That everything ends with an ear of wheat.

Epitaph

Here may you sleep,
In the smell of paper
Inscribed with difficulty
And barely intelligible,
Too delicate god of the temple
Called childhood –
Whole sacrifices
And quarters of mistake.

Here may you sleep,
Buried in rhymes
Which you can
No longer hear,
Involuntary saint
And entirely
Among craven bishops
And cruel angels.

Here may you sleep,
At peace and dreaming,
Apotheosis
Of who knows how many Jobs,
Passed through prisons
And flames meekly
Towards a paradise
Of potato-sugar.

Here may you sleep,
Displaced a second time,
May the letter's dust be light upon you.

I Breathe, I Breathe

I breathe, I breathe
As I lie with eyes closed,
Feel the stars sharp through my eyelids
Writing soft signs on my retina
Like dead fish on the glitter of the water.
It happens as in a dream – I breathe, I breathe,
The vault of thick glass is about to break
When the frozen blood of evening stars
Swallows it up and overflows,
And then the lingering creak of light,
Like gravel under the snout of the hoe,
And your footsteps as they move away echo
The muffled sound of chimes under waters
Advancing so transparently
Almost unseen – closer and closer still;
It happens as in a dream – I breathe, I breathe
The crystal that's about to bury me.

How I Could Have Wished

How I could have wished all
To be perfect as a plant
Which only the late fall
Has the power to snuff out
And over which a snowfall
Has the luck to snow
The next life.

How I could have wished
Us to be like no others,
Beautiful and pure
To know nothing of strife,
To pass through the world
Strangers to lies,
Amazed at suffering,
Happy to arrive together
In the next life.

How I could have wished
Us always to be equals,
Young forever sliding on a slope
At the end of which, damp, deep
May the moon reflect
In the next life.

How I could have wished.
We have lost
Just one high moment, enough
For hatred to splatter us
With death,

And to roll us both far, far away
Together,
Alone and so old
That we wouldn't recognize each other
Even if we met again
In the next life.

Lights and Shadows

A net of shadows
Has caught me and holds me
And I can't escape
Since I don't know what blade
Can cut it;
My handcuffs are
Of mist,
But who can manage
To bend them?

My eyes are bound
With a strip of dusk
Reddened over the water,
Around me the walls
Are transparent and soft,
The living body could almost walk through them.

But everything is accident –
I'm free or not
Depending on how the light falls through clouds,
Beautiful or not
Depending on the way
A branch of a tree sways
Now and then
And I'm loved, in accordance with
The petals of a flower.

Between light and shadow,
Prisoner and fulfilment,
Like a gull
Between sea and sky.
All that depends on me
Is the radiance
Of this smile
That gags me.

Waiting

Every word is a jar
Almost full of alcohol:
Some drink it;
Some disinfect their wounds with it;
Others shake it in the light and cloud it,
Making the dregs and silt rise;
Some line the flagons up
In the order of their size,
Playing soldiers with them;
Some group them
By colours, or by shapes;
Others uncork them
To release the alcohol
Or to try it out amazed
Setting it alight.

I don't do anything.
I sit and wait
To remind myself
Of the fruit
From which I distilled it.
What was it like?

Twins

Twins in the uterus of fear,
Inhabitants of the same cell,
Blind and dumb
In the darkness savagely resonant
Only with the nourishing pulse,
Tearing us from invertebrates,
From fish and from birds, from beasts,
To give us birth
In her own image and likeness.

Without right of appeal
Sentenced to birth,
Alone and helpless in the face
Of our growth wrapped up
In its growing body
As in a tomb that leavens the life to come.
We two,
Twins in the uterus of fear.

Sun of Insomnia

Sun of insomnia,
White melted metal,
Unbearable to the retina,
Going through the eyelid,
Blinding unsleep,
Glance without hope of shadow
Keeping me suspended
High, above all senses,
Above the darkness, sweet,
Promiscuous and hellish,
In the most pitiless, indecent
Light
From which I long just
To fall, to fall . . .

Late

It is too late:
The very cell unravels,
I no longer recognize any pact –
The sunset is rancid
And the sunrise faked.
A star of prey lies in wait
For the moment of supreme radiance
In the sky acid as a whimper
Dissolving curses;

But the ray is getting dusty
And the wind scatters it,
Heaps of luminous sand
Drift through nooks.
It is too late:
Bright sky, if it exists, is just theft,
When the clouds display
The viscera of heaven

With a shamelessness that exorcizes loves.
Indifferent to itself, the cell unravels,
The light dries up from its own power
Over the deserted universe,
When the scream is death,
Silence is infamous
And the pitch-dark has thin roots
In too late.

Inflation of Birds

Nest in which birds, often
Foreign, lay their eggs,
With the right at most
To choose the bird,
But not the destiny of the nest,
In your annals
There has been inscribed
Since the making of the world
No revolt
Against this universe
Even more
Fated to bankruptcy
As a result of
The inflation of birds.

Inside

A flight unstopped but rarely
Between two anniversaries,
Just so that you can catch breath
In order to run again,
A flight into sleep, into silence,
Into books, into alcohol,
It doesn't matter where,
Into hatred, into love,
All that matters is that it be
As complete as possible;
A flight into yourself as deep as can be,
From the outside, from the calendar,
So that nothing can be seen
But a moss-covered back at most
Or, when the wind blows,
Two palms, moving,
Striking against each other without conviction;
A flight without stopping,
Always inside,
Always deeper, more fetid,
And everything known for millennia,
The beautiful millennia of yesteryear
When we were running in the woods . . .
Now, only into our own entrails.

Courage

I look at my hands:
Twiglets on which
Never have eyelids
Of leaves blinked;
Wing-points on which
Feathers have never
Dared to grow;
And not so much as a claw
Managed, at the tips,
To sprout like some
Delicate bud of a beast.
I look at my hands
As at letters which
Don't have the courage
To form by themselves
One word.

With My Face Toward the Mountains

If I were to stop hearing,
Would the world seem suddenly ridiculous
Like a broadcast with the sound cut off
On television?
A deaf God
Over whom the waters become woollen and fall,
And the clouds collide without thunder
Like balls of lavatory paper
In the rubbish-bin of the sky,
Would give the signal to halt the sense
Of this universe that only exists
Through the screeching produced.
And his great palms,
Which sometimes amplify
The pavilion of his ear,
Would place themselves on my shoulders
Turning me slowly
With my face toward the mountains.

The Father

It is not I who decide.
Atoms become sand,
Sand grows into gravel,
Gravel turns into letters,
Letters sprout, burst into bud,
Yield words,
The words become animals, mate
And give birth.
It is not I who decide.
Never
When I see a pregnant word,
Do I know who the father is.

Star Borne on the Wind

From the beginning you were borne on the wind
Like a seed.
I even joked: 'Who's ever seen
A star borne on the wind?'
But later,
When you settled on my forehead
And began to sprout,
I understood that you *are* a seed.
Greedy, savagely stuck into my brain,
With harsh rays imagining roots,
You are a seed.
What a pity
That the plant which,
Light from light, you bear
Cannot be seen
Until after
I have gone into the dark.

My Eye

My eye is
An animal
That long ago ceased
To be omnivorous.
In the beginning
It made do with little:
A few boughs, a few leaves,
A flower, a stem.
Then it moved on to essences
And only corns, grains, seeds
Roused its interest
And appetite for sense.
And now it simply refuses
To swallow a thing,
It clenches its eyelashes like teeth
Terrified by themselves
And no longer accepts anything,
Shouting that it has everything it needs inside.
Enormous quantities of provisions
Which it devours with greed,
As witness the tears that drop now and then
From closed eyelids
Like saliva dribbling indecent and senile . . .

Gathering Angels

... Now and then
A muffled plop
Like the fall
Of a fruit onto grass.
How time goes by!
Angels
Have ripened and started dropping:
It's autumn in heaven too ...

The Bell I Hear

The bell I hear
Tolls so far away,
I can't tell whether
Through earth, through sky or water
Its voice
Passes, like an animal
Tired of death,
Dragging itself one more
Yard into the burrow-grave
Able to conceal and contain it,
In the frightened hideout
That I am,
In which it dies
Every time
Before saying
Where the bell is,
Whose it is and why
It started to toll . . .

Letters

This fear of flowing
From A,
Never towards A,
This fear
Of going through
All the letters
That you know beforehand
From the others
Who've been through them
As they had their chance,
As far as Q, as far as T,
The happiest as far as Z,
But not one
Ever returned,
Not one able
To jump back
Over A,
Not one able to imagine even
What's before
Or after the end of the alphabet:
More letters?
More letters?
More letters?

Calcium Molecules

I mustn't hurry,
I must let time pass,
Each second as it falls
Erodes suffering
A little bit.
I must wait.
Each wave that breaks
Chips at the rock
To which I'm chained,
Each grain of rust
Thins the chain.
In a millennium, in two,
The rock will be sand,
The iron of the rings dust,
My bones calcium molecules
Scattered on water,
Suffering nothing.

Alone

He is the one alone
Not because, among them all,
He is the true one,
But because
The core of them all is the same.
In the leaves of the oak,
In the entrails of birds,
In the hare-in-the-moon,
In bread and wine,
He is the one alone.
So alone
That he gets bored stiff
And comes alive.

Pattern

Oh, the flight of the lonely one
Towards the one alone,
After the pattern of which
Springs flow
And avalanches form –
How much fear and how much heroism,
How much loneliness.
When it moves away from me
I follow it
Ready for anything,
Breathless.
When it comes back,
Frightened I hide
And try to disappear.
The flight of the lonely one
From and towards
The centre of loneliness,
After the pattern of which
Seas make waves.

The Cold Melt

Entire decades waiting for
The turning of the key in the lock;
More and more rusted,
Lying in wait for entire decades
Without words,
Without a destiny.
From time to time,
Seeming to move a little,
And then,
Oh, the division into voices
According to the illusion of movement:
Those to whom it seemed
To have turned forwards,
Those to whom it seemed
To have turned backwards,
Those to whom even lack of movement
Seems a trump . . .
Who and what could stop
The chimera?
But no,
Only the progress of rust
To the heart of iron,
The cold melt,
Molecule by molecule
The red dust replacing the bolt
(And again, the chorus of signs,
Suppositions, opinions:
In a century, in two,
In a millennium . . .)
History in slow motion.

Scene

Six or seven
With snouts clenched
On the same prey,
With bodies, hallucinatorily
Elongated by tails,
Laid out radially
On the asphalt,
Had formed a sun
With fat, trembling rays,
Risen from the ditch.
Sun of rats
In an asphalt sky,
Apollo of the trash, a future
Star with fur for another
Age of basements and gutters
Drained towards doomsday,
A rodent god
Ravenous from the years
With haloes
Of trash . . .

Ballad

I have no other Ana,
Build myself into the wall,
Yet who can tell me this is enough
When the wall does not tumble
By itself,
But pushed by the whim
Of a sleepwalking bulldozer
Advancing through the nightmare in a heap.
And again I build
As if I built a wave,
The second day again,
The third day again,
The fourth day again,
An eternally liquid monastery
Fated to crumble at the shore;
Again I build, oh, lime
And brick
And, without stain,
A being
As reinforcement
To the infamous dream:
I have no other Ana
And myself even
Less and less often
Do I have.

Baladă

N-am altă Ană,
Mă zidesc pe mine,
Dar cine-mi poate spune că-i destul
Cînd zidul nu se surpă
De la sine,
Ci-mpins de-o toană
De buldozer somnambul
Înaintînd de-a valma prin coşmar.
Şi iar zidesc
Cum aş zidi un val,
A doua zi iar,
A treia zi iar,
A patra zi iar,
O mănăstire pururea lichidă
Sortită să se năruie la mal;
Şi iar zidesc, o, var
Şi cărămidă
Şi, fără de prihană,
O făptură
Ca armătură
Visului infam:
N-am altă Ană
Şi pe mine chiar
Din ce în ce mai rar
Mă am.

Postscript

AFTER THE EXTRAORDINARY EVENTS of December 1989 in Romania, something, however inadequate, must be said. In one of the four protest poems whose surprise publication in *Amfiteatru* (December 1984) led to her second banning, Ana Blandiana wrote: 'I believe that we are a vegetal people / Why otherwise the stillness / In which we await defoliation? / ... / Who has ever seen / A tree in revolt?' We now know how suddenly and at what terrible cost a people's apparently resigned, abject suffering can explode. The revolt which began in Timişoara had overturned forty-two years of communist rule and twenty-four years of nightmarish, medieval tyranny in some ten days. Or so it seemed in that euphoric moment. Unfortunately subsequent events have shown that old authoritarian habits die hard. With Ana Blandiana's permission, we dedicate *The Hour of Sand* to the memory of all who died and suffered in the cause of Romania's freedom.

This book is still a product of the age of the dictatorship and the long arm of Ceauşescu's repression and censorship. The December uprising took place between the printing of the first edition's cover and of its text. For fear of making Ana Blandiana's life in Bucharest more difficult than it had been, our Introduction could only hint at the nature of the 'direct threat' to her country's fabric and values, or at the 'circumstances beyond her control' which caused her third banning in autumn 1988. But we decided not to change it, since it focuses on values rather than on circumstances, which are likely to be unsettled for some time.

Our selection of poems would have been no different had we begun to prepare the book now, except that we might have included more poems from her delayed collection *The Architecture of Waves*, which surfaced in spring 1990, and her remarkable protest poem 'Everything'. This appeared in an anonymous translation with commentary in *The Independent* of 18 February 1989, and in *The Chatto Book of Cabbages and Kings*, ed. Francis Spufford (1989). That version and its notes, with those of the other three *Amphitheatre* poems, were made in 1986 by Peter Jay and Andrei Brezianu, and are now included in this second edition's Appendix. Extensive documentation on the treatment of protesting Romanian writers under Ceauşescu can be found in *Index on Censorship* for September 1989, which also contains a version of the children's poem which led to the ban on Ana Blandiana in 1988.

Ana Blandiana is at heart an apolitical writer whom the times – past and present – forced into a political rôle. She was one of several writers and artists co-opted onto the original Council for National Salvation, which secured and directed the revolution from the Bucharest television headquarters. By early in January she had already found it necessary to distance herself from the Council's manoeuvrings, and she resigned as soon as she realized that she was being used to lend respectability to undemocratic practices. Thus she was forced back into her rôle as a dissident. Throughout the period leading up to the elections of 20 May she made clear, both in her articles and by her presence, her support for the democratic ideals of the University Square demonstrators. She addressed the crowd on several occasions.

'At least things were quiet under Ceauşescu', said someone to a Bucharest University friend of ours shortly after the infamous assault by miners on the demonstrators and their sympathizers. It was lucky for Ana Blandiana that she was out of the country in mid-June: one woman in Bucharest was certainly mistaken for her and badly beaten by the miners, and rumours say that they beat not one woman but two. Embraced as a symbol by the *golani* and hated by those who connive in defending 'democracy' by brutal means, those who preach but actually fear freedom of expression,

Ana Blandiana faces this 'new' old situation with hope and serenity, convinced that in the days ahead the social rôle of writers through journalism and creative work will remain strong.

Over the years, Romanians have looked to the arts to help them survive oppression, to preserve the spark of truth and the hope of freedom. Despite intimidation and censorship, writers and artists have performed this task with courage and subtlety. It will be a long time before there is any semblance of what we in the west regard as normal literary or artistic life. Meanwhile, we can take heart from the example that writers have set, and even from the leading rôle they have played in the preservation of civilized human values, the sustenance of their people under dictatorship, and the support they have given to the cause of freedom. May it begin to take root in a democratic Romania.

PETER JAY
ANCA CRISTOFOVICI

June 1990

Appendix: The *Amphitheatre* Poems

Two of these poems need some explanation. 'Children's Crusade' was aimed at the legislation outlawing abortion, first enacted in 1966 but only seriously enforced from about 1983 in order to make progress towards Ceauşescu's target of doubling the population (then static, or even in decline) by the end of the century. Four children per family was the aim. Contraceptives were unobtainable.

Many couples had privately concluded that Romania was no place in which to bring up children. But childlessness was penalized, and child-bearing rewarded, through taxation. Doctors and patients alike who defied the anti-abortion laws faced heavy fines or imprisonment. Most remarkably, all working women had to submit to regular gynaecological checkups, carried out by squads of doctors visiting factories and offices. It was their job to ensure that pregnancies were neither concealed nor terminated.

'Everything' would mean little to non-Romanians without a detailed commentary. Happily, many of the circumstances referred to in the notes, written by Peter Jay and Andrei Brezianu in 1986, have now changed. But the commentary would lose much of its point by being updated, if that were possible. The poem is an inventory of things which either did or didn't exist, an index of the possibilities and impossibilities of everyday Romanian life. It is built around two categories, setting up a counterpoint between them: (*a*) the things or goods that occupied the forefront of people's daily attention in their need to survive or to divert themselves from that need; (*b*) the symbols of the state apparatus, the charades of the personality cult and its trappings – the things with which people were constantly bombarded in propaganda.

Children's Crusade

A whole population
Not yet born
But condemned to birth
Marshalled in columns before birth
Foetus next to foetus.
A whole population
That neither sees nor hears nor understands
But marches forward
Through the writhing bodies of women
Through the blood
Of unconsulted mothers.

Everything

... Leaves, words, tears
Tinned food, cats
Trams from time to time, queues for flour
Weevils, empty bottles, speeches
Elongated images on the TV
Colorado beetles, petrol
Pennants, the European Cup
Trucks with gas cylinders, well-known portraits
Export-reject apples
Newspapers, loaves
Blended oil, carnations
Receptions at the airport
Cico-cola, balloons
Bucharest salami, diet yoghurt
Gipsy women with Kents, Crevedia eggs
Rumours
The Saturday serial, coffee substitutes
The struggle of nations for peace, choirs
Production by the acre
Gerovital, the Victory Street lads
The Hymn to Romania, Adidas shoes
Bulgarian stewed fruit, jokes, ocean fish
Everything.

Limitations

We plants
Are not protected from illness
Or from madness
(Haven't you ever seen a plant
Lose its mind
And put its buds back in the earth?)
Or from hunger
Or from fear
Or from prison
(Haven't you ever seen a yellowing
Stem strung up to the bars?)
The one and only thing we are protected from
(Perhaps deprived of)
Is escape.

I Believe

I believe that we are a vegetal people
Why otherwise the stillness
In which we await defoliation?
Why the courage
To let ourselves slide on the toboggan of sleep
Almost to death's door
In the certainty
That we shall reach the point of being born
All over again?
I believe that we are a vegetal people.
Who has ever seen
A tree in revolt?

Notes on 'Everything'

The title is the first irony. 'Totul' (everything) is a catchphrase or verbal tic which punctuates every other sentence of Ceauşescu's speeches. He uses it either to insist that everything remains to be done by, or that the Party has done everything conceivable for, the people. 'Everything' is a fit symbol for a bankrupt regime, the nature of which is to insist that it has the answer to everything.

1 *Leaves* can be seen on trees. There is no shortage of *words* and *tears*.

2 *Tinned*, not fresh food which is harder to find. Self-service or corner grocery stores used to offer row on row of dusty tins (fish, stewed or pickled vegetables) which would be long past their sell-by dates if they had them. They are thin on the shelves now.

Cats: The State enterprise *Ecarisajul* battles with some success against stray dogs, but has less luck with cats. Bucharest gossip has immortalized a certain cat which challenged the General Secretary's dogs, as he was surveying the district where his grandiose Civic Centre now nears completion. As he approached the Brâncoveanu Hospital, founded in the eighteenth century, his way was barred by an alley cat which proceeded to wound his two watchdogs in the ensuing scrap. He ordered the cat to be caught and brought to him. Naturally, this proved impossible, thereby vindicating the proverb 'A cat may look at a King'.

The good cat, alas, failed to save the historic quarter beyond the Piata Unirii market from destruction. 40,000 residents were evacuated for the clearance of the site, fine old houses, churches, monastery, Brâncoveanu Hospital and all.

3 *Trams from time to time*, but they are so full that you can't get on them.

Queues for flour and everything else: bread, sugar, eggs, bits of non-export or -restaurant grade meat, vodka, you name it.

4 *Empty bottles* are kept, either to reclaim your deposit, or because unless you bring your own bottles you cannot buy

various liquid goods, such as cooking oil. The energy shortage has either closed the bottle factories or reduced their output to a trickle. 'Empty bottles' is also a familiar street-cry by which gypsy women, collecting bottles for recycling, announce their passage. The prudent citizen always carries an empty bottle or two, just in case there is a queue worth joining somewhere along the way.

Speeches are never in short supply, and are never short.

5 *Elongated images on the TV*: things are enlarged and distorted by the poor quality of the sets or of their reception.

6 *Petrol*: strictly rationed and very expensive. Private use of cars is also banned during the worst months of winter, January to March, a restriction imposed shortly after the publication of this poem and now enforced annually.

7 *The European Cup*: football, at least, is politically uncontroversial. There may be little *panem* but there are some *circenses*.

8 *Trucks with gas cylinders* are eagerly awaited by households which rely on butane gas cylinders for their stoves. The ration is one cylinder every two months. Perhaps irrelevantly, the phrase also brings to mind the common sight in Bucharest streets of the buses which were adapted to run on on gas: they sport huge cylindrical tanks which run the length of the bus's roof, marked GAZ. Unfortunately the engineers had been unable to find an economical method of converting the engines, so the roof-tanks are passengers.

Well-known portraits: you know who. Icons of the Big C. Compulsory in offices, factories, etc.

9 *Export-reject apples*: all food of decent quality is now exported. Romania has halved its foreign hard-currency debt in the last five or six years by exporting everything worth buying.

10 *Newspapers*: well, yes, in a manner of speaking. Their main use is as wrapping paper.

Loaves sell like hot cakes.

11 *Blended oil* is the euphemism for adulterated cooking oil.

Carnations abound, and are handy for

12 *Receptions at the airport*. These are frequent, since he likes to entertain, and require the clearance of main streets for

the convoy of official cars which sweep visiting dignitaries into the capital, past the new mock marble (hardboard) arch, which dwarfs the old replica of the Arc de Triomphe, and on which is writ large: THE AGE OF NICOLAE CEAUŞESCU 1965–1985: A GOLDEN AGE ('Epocă de aur'), and finally down the boulevard which has been festively lined with dragooned schoolchildren waving *pennants* (line 7).

13   *Cico*, to give it its simple Romanian name, is an acidic, urine-coloured soft drink, universally available when all else fails. It is palatable.

14   *Bucharest* (or 'summer') *salami* is less so, but almost all the excellent Sibiu ('winter') salami goes for export. The Bucharest version is a generic name for a substance produced nation-wide to a recipe given the official seal of approval by the General Secretary. Contents may include powdered bones, soya oil, scraps of meat and skin, and the offal or worse of various animals, especially of coypu. Even shortages of toilet paper have been attributed to changes in the recipe. It imparts the characteristically acrid odour which greets the entrant to what used to be called delicatessens.

Diet yoghurt, i.e. ordinary yoghurt considered as a health-food, is good but you had to queue for it at the crack of dawn. It is now unobtainable.

15   *Kent* cigarettes are a second currency: why only Kents should have attained this status is a mystery. The *cachet* of Kent has no rival. They are also the secret police's favoured brand. On the black market, three cartons will fetch the average monthly salary; a single packet changes hands for 100 lei. The gypsy *mafiosi* are thought to be the main Kent smugglers, and their women-folk are involved in its distribution. Kents are confiscated at customs from Romanians returning home. As in ancient Greece, it was a custom at Romanian funerals for a coin to be placed in the dead person's mouth. The new custom is: a packet of Kent on the corpse's chest.

Crevedia eggs: eggs from the Crevedia state farm are supposed to be the best, and attract large queues when rumours of a supply circulate.

16   *Rumours* are the most reliable source of information about what's going on and where things might be obtained.

17   *The Saturday serial*: the weekly treat of imported TV;
Dallas, *The Avengers*, *Columbo*, *Kojak*. From time to time the
authorities have tried to drop these in favour of home-made
patriotic drama, but they have succumbed for once to the
pressure of public opinion.

Coffee substitutes: real coffee can only be obtained at the
'shops', the Romanian term for hard-currency stores in hotel
lobbies. (Oil, sugar and flour are now on sale in 'shops'.) The
coffee-drinking population now has to make do with blends of
acorn, chicory and so on, since coffee is too expensive and
luxurious to import. Visitors from Hungary, where coffee is
easily bought, are searched for smuggled coffee.

18   *The struggle of nations for peace* is the Conducator's
rallying cry. The only political demonstrations permitted are
those which he organizes against the nuclear threat. This wins
him friends abroad, or used to.

Choirs grace such occasions. They are also seen on TV
when the screen is not occupied by football, the Saturday serial
or – speeches.

19   *Production by the acre*: much mention of this stirs the
peasantry to its patriotic duty of increasing produce.

20   *Gerovital* is Dr Ana Aslan's elixir, now marketed
abroad in the state's pursuit of hard currency. It is regarded as a
ludicrous emblem of the state's belief in the gullibility of
western consumers. (But it seems to fool a lot of Romanians.)

The Victory Street lads – or just 'the lads', 'the boys' – are the
secret police's plain-clothes heavies, entrusted with guarding
the President's route into the centre. They are thought to be an
elite corps of hand-picked orphans. Easy to spot by their suits.
There is no shortage of them, but they are expensive to buy.

21   *The Hymn to Romania* is the much advertised, all-year-
round 'festival', a series of amateurish artistic events – music,
dance and theatre – whose purpose seems to be twofold: (1) to
give constant, ritual praise to the Party and especially its leader,
and (2) to provide lowbrow, *kitsch* but patriotic performances as
an antidote to the ideologically suspect, real professional thing.

Adidas shoes have been trendy in our label-conscious
western society. That guarantees their status in Romania,
where they are manufactured under licence and are, naturally,

in short supply. However, there is a nicely macabre twist to the term in colloquial usage, which has it that pigs' trotters – sometimes available as an alternative to the now rare (because exported) pork which used to be plentiful in restaurants, and less scarce than other meat at the butchers – are the slaughtered pigs' Adidases.

22 *Bulgarian stewed fruit* was permanently available in 1984, having been dumped on the Romanian market years before. It has all gone now.

Jokes galore. You cannot spend more than five minutes in conversation, even with an official, without hearing several of the latest. They are sometimes grimly funny.

Ocean fish, much promoted for its nutritional qualities, is a euphemism for stale frozen fish of suspect, greyish appearance and dubious gastric consequences.

23 *Everything*: and There Is No Alternative, just more of Everything.

1986

Romanian Poetry from Anvil

NINA CASSIAN
Life Sentence
Edited and introduced by William Jay Smith

This large selection of poetry by Romania's most distinguished poet in exile spans forty-five years, and includes translations by such poets as Stanley Kunitz, Richard Wilbur, Carolyn Kizer, William Jay Smith, Fleur Adcock and Dana Gioia. Nina Cassian has lived in the USA since 1985.

'Nina Cassian is a world-class poet, high-spirited, fierce, intelligent, uncompromising, and wonderfully nervy ... a writer at the peak of her power.'

— STANLEY KUNITZ

ŞTEFAN AUG. DOINAŞ
Alibi and other poems
Translated by Peter Jay & Virgil Nemoianu

A selection of twenty lyric and allegorical poems, introducing an outstanding contemporary poet, critic and translator. Doinaş, born in 1922, studied under Lucian Blaga at the University of Cluj. He lives in Bucharest and is an editor of the magazine devoted to world literature, *Secolul 20*.

NICHITA STĂNESCU
The Still Unborn About the Dead
Translated by Peter Jay & Petru Popescu

A representative selection of poems by the writer generally considered as Romania's greatest and most influential recent poet. He lived from 1933 to 1983. The book includes many of his lyric poems and his major sequence *Eleven Elegies*.